CU00240698

How To Be The Next Top Model

2nd Edition

19 Secrets Revealed By A Professional Modeling Instructor That You Must Know To Succeed In Modeling

Colleen M. Jansen

How To Be The Next Top Model

Publisher: Enlightened Publishing

ISBN-13: 978-1507888957

ISBN-10: 1507888953

Disclaimer

The Publisher has strived to be as accurate and complete as possible in the creation of this book. While all attempts have been made to verify information provided in this publication, the Publisher assumes no responsibility for errors, omissions, or contrary interpretation of the subject matter herein. Any perceived slights of specific persons, peoples, or organizations are unintentional.

This book is not intended for use as a source of legal, business, accounting or financial advice. All readers are advised to seek services of competent professionals in the legal, business, accounting, and finance fields.

The information in this book is not intended or implied to be a substitute for professional medical advice, diagnosis or treatment. All content contained in this book is for general information purposes only. Always consult your healthcare provider before carrying on any health program.

Table of Contents

Introduction

Welcome to the super exciting world of modeling! If you have been wondering what it takes to be the next Marilyn Monroe, Tyra Banks, or Claudia Schiffer, you will soon learn all about it.

This book will tell you what you need to do in order to network, put together a portfolio, book shoots, and even get signed with an illustrious agency. It will go over topics such as how to promote yourself, the different types of modeling, and personal things that you can do in order to improve yourself. By the end of this, you will have a basic understanding on how to be a successful model, and some great foundations to build yourself on.

It's very easy to see why so many men, women, and children dream of being models. Anyone who has seen a single episode of *America's Next Top Model* can tell you why this is the case. The world of modeling has everything that makes a Hollywood dream complete – glamour, fame, money, high fashion, and of course, popularity. Modeling is one of the most popular careers that young women partake in. Parents of said women also encourage it as well, and some will pay for expensive schools. You get all the fun of being paid to stand around and be photographed by numerous people, and if you become really big, you will even get to be on the cover of popular magazines. It's a way of fame that many yearn for, but it's a road that isn't all sunshine and rainbows all the time. It's a road of hard work and dedication.

The world of modeling is fraught with pitfalls, problems, and all sorts of different things that can trip up even an experienced model. As a professional modeling instructor, I have seen it all. Many men/women who want to be models end up failing due to the fact that they don't know how to prepare themselves. There are ways to improve yourself and become a better model than you expected yourself to be. Modeling can be hard. Many times you are going to want to cry out in frustration. But remember to always keep your eyes on the prize.

Take the tips I offer to heart; and you won't have to deal with half of the stuff that many unfortunate newbies will have to deal with. Newbies in this industry have it hard, and if you are not careful, you might fall into the trap as well. However, I have made this book clear and concise so that you will be able to effectively model yourself with my advice.

With the invention of the Internet, the world of modeling has suddenly opened up, allowing people of all ages to try their hand at this glamorous pass time and career option. Some has gotten famous off of just being Internet models, and it's a means that is becoming popular.

Now is the time that you should be chasing your dreams. The sooner you start, the sooner you can get your first taste of the glitz, the glam, and the world of modeling. It's time you grab life by the horns. What are you waiting for? Start reading!

Chapter 1: So You Want To Be A Model?

Modeling is a glamorous career, a great hobby, and almost everyone can find a niche that fits their style. If you have been considering becoming a model, then start looking into the different kinds of modeling that you can specialize in before you start working on a portfolio.

A portfolio that fits with the niche that you are going into is key. Many make the mistake of trying to hit all of the different niches at once, and their portfolio looks like a jumbled mess of pictures. Instead, when you are making a portfolio, make sure to separate them into different categories. When you are going for a casting call, you can then cater to that type of modeling with your pictures, instead of showing them a whole slew that might not have anything to do with it.

It is also important to think of one genre that you want to specialize in. Commonly, many people think that they can go straight for the Tyra Banks modeling, but that's far from the truth. You need to build yourself up, and if you are not a certain body size or height, you will not be able to get into that. The world of modeling is changing though, and standards are evolving. It is important to give yourself a realistic goal so you don't disappoint yourself. This way, you can market yourself according to what the market in your area of specialization wants.

The different types of modeling are as follows:

- **High Fashion** - This form of modeling is one of the most difficult to get into, as well as one of the most difficult to stay in. High fashion models have to be very tall, and very, very thin. Most high fashion models are 5'10 or over, and can weigh as little as 110 pounds.

  This is the type of modeling that you see on TV, the modeling that allows women to flock the catwalk, sporting the various designs that were created. You not only have to meet the criteria, but also have to have perfect skin, perfect hair, and be able to rock these ridiculous fashions. You will be subjected to wearing different outfits that are normally not your style, and you will also have to be skillful in wearing heels that could give you monstrous height.

Ideally, high fashion models can wear a size 0 through 4. High fashion models also have to be very young in order to be hired. Modeling agencies start hiring models as young as 13 years old for the high fashion world. The oldest hires can be as old as 23 years old; however, this is very rare. These models usually last until they are in their late 20's and early 30's, and then they are usually unable to do this type of modeling due to the aging of the body and the slowing of the metabolism.

High fashion models are a very high-paid form of modeling, and can be seen on the runways of Paris every year. They also get much more fame, exposure, and magazine work than other models. If you are shooting for this, then you will want to start off early and make sure you are perfect for it.

- **Fashion Models** - Fashion models is a wider category than high fashion. Regular fashion models can still do runway, and can also do print ads. Proportionality is a key factor to who gets chosen to be a fashion model. Usually this proportionality is determined by what the person wants. For example, if a woman has a longer set of legs, they might be chosen to do print ads and some runway that has short skirts and shorts. If you have a longer torso, there might be more print ads for clothing that flatters that.

  Fashion models can be a little bit shorter than high fashion models, and they can start at 5'5. Fashion models, similar to high fashion models, need to be leggy. Though there are curvy fashion models, they often don't get as much work as those who have a more slender silhouette.

- **Plus Size Models** - Plus size models are actually some of the most high-paid

models in the industry. They are needed in commercials, runways, and print
ads. It has become a popular niche in
recent years. With the normal weight of
the human body becoming larger, more
women want ads to represent them. A
woman who is plus-sized will listen
more to a woman who is around their
size than a model who is 110 pounds
and is wearing a miniskirt. It's used to
cater to this new niche, and it allows
more women to enter the modeling industry.

Plus size models need to be tall, and
most of them are over 5'10. Plus size
modeling traditionally starts at size 10
or size 12. However, due to the size
shift in the fashion world, plus size
models can be as thin as size 6.

Modeling agencies look for women
who have perfect skin and teeth, and
very pretty features. Much like regular
fashion models, they need to be propor-
tionate. This means that you can have a
curvy figure, but you cannot have a
figure that is disproportionately large
in one part or another.

- **Fit Models** - Models who can fit into sample size clothing are called fit models. They are used behind-the-scenes in order to help designers create clothes that everyone can wear. They are used in order to help make alterations, and to show off how it will look before putting it on the runway model.

  Fit models are well-paid, and can be a lot older than regular fashion models. Most fit models need to sign with an agency in order to get work. Fit models can be plus sized, or standard sized. They don't need to have perfect skin, teeth, and hair in order to do this though.

- **Cosmetic and Hair Models** - Models who specialize in these areas need to have long, thick, healthy hair, and great skin. They are used to model different hair and makeup styles, and are usually with the makeup artist for hours before showing off the results.

  The models who are most successful in this field have unique features, but can still market their look to mainstream

organizations. There is no height minimum, but models who are runway
height still tend to get more work than
others.

- **Parts Models** - Parts models are models
  who have very beautiful parts of their
  body. The most common parts models
  get their jobs in hand and foot modeling, but there are other fields that require parts models as well.

  Parts models don't need to show off
  their entire body when they are modeling, but instead the camera will only
  target these specific areas of the body.
  Parts models can increase their chances
  of getting hired by having acting experience or working as fashion models.

- **Promo Models** - Promotional models
  work to promote products at live
  events. There is no height requirement,
  but having a winning personality and
  smile helps. Many times these women
  might have to wear skimpier clothing,
  and they will have to show off their
  body in order to promote things. If you
  want to go into this, make sure to tone

up your body and make sure your personality matches it as well.

- **Glamour Models** - Swimsuit, lingerie, and pinup models all fit under the category of glamour models. In this genre, models who have curvy bodies are welcomed with open arms.

  Due to the fact that glamour models aren't used for runway or fit modeling, they often can be much shorter than their fashion counterparts. This type of modeling is the easiest to get into, and if you are wondering if you are fit for a modeling career, this is a great place to start. It's the lowest paying of them all, but some still make it big. It's a niche that many women can get into as long as they look pretty and have a decent body. If your dream is to be on a calendar, this is the genre for you!

Of course, there are plenty of other types of modeling out there for you to try. Try to find a genre of modeling that works for your look. Go for the ones that best fit your lifestyle. If you are older, it might be best that you don't try to go into runway modeling. You can start off trying to go into glamour modeling in order to get some shoots. From there, you will be able to get more work and become more successful.

Check all of the genres out before you decide to start your career in the world of modeling; after all, everybody has something beautiful about them.

Chapter 2: Modeling Agencies

If you are an aspiring model, you will need to find a way to get new gigs, find new contacts, and network. Being a freelance model has many pitfalls – rude photographers, a lack of a screening process, and lower wages. It's important to know that you will probably encounter all of these things when you are starting out, not just because of the fact that this is the world we live in, but because it comes with the job.

Due to the issues that many models experience, many of them choose to work with a modeling agency in order to bypass all these problems. Modeling agencies have the connections that models normally don't, and they also have the negotiating power that makes them very attractive for girls who want to pursue a career.

Modeling agencies also have a knack for creating a whole marketing approach for each model, branding them as their own special persona. Not all modeling agencies are alike. Some agencies will work harder for their models, while others have more connections that give them access to more jobs.

There are also fake agencies out there that want you to give them money, only to have no return back. If you fall for one of these, you are not only going to feel bummed, but these scammers could take and use your personal information. Always check the credentials of the place first before you even bother to go there.

In order to get the best amount of work that you can get as a model, it is crucial to try to sign with one of the top modeling agencies. Here are a few examples of these agencies:

- **Wilhelmina, NYC** is one of the best modeling agencies on the East Coast. Famous for not letting their models get taken advantage of, Wilhelmina is an agency that is known for class, poise, and sophistication. However, Wilhelmina is also the target of a very terrible scam due to name theft and misspellings. Make sure you sign with the right one before you start working.

- **Ford** is the name that models, photographers, and fashion designers admire the most. Most of the top models in the industry, including several supermodels, have signed with this illustrious agency.

- **IKON** is a good place to start your modeling career if you are into the more edgy looks. This agency is quite famous for being protective of the models who work for it, and also is known for being able to market models for their best shots at showbiz. If you have a penchant for acting or want to get into acting, then this is a great agency to sign with.

- **Elite** has branches on both the East and the West coasts, and also is known for being one of the top names for fashion and commercial modeling. Elite models are often spotted on Paris runways, New York fashion shows, and other similar events.

Be forewarned. Joining a modeling agency isn't as easy as many would have you believe. Most agencies are very harsh when it comes to telling hopefuls whether or not they make it in. They won't try to sugarcoat things – if they think you are too heavy, they will tell you straight to your face. Their screenings are also hard, so make sure that you are ready to be put to work when you get there. They want their models to earn the fame that they desire, so be ready for that. Another thing that really makes the top modeling agencies an ivory tower that most models will not be able to enter is that their physical requirements are extremely rigid, and exceptions are almost never made.

Typical Requirements of Top Agencies

In order to sign with a top agency, you will need to fit into a height requirement. Typically, female models have to be at the very least, 5'9 in order to get people interested in signing you. Male models have to be around 6'1. For "regular" female models, you will have to be a size 00-4. Plus size models start at size 8. This doesn't take into account the near-perfect hair, skin, and features that models need to have.

Age is also a major factor when it comes to getting signed with a top modeling agency. If you are a tall, awkward, gangly teenage girl, you will be snatched up almost immediately. In fact, modeling scouts start looking for runway models as young as 13 years old for the Paris runways.

Ladies who are over 22 or 23 will have a much, much harder time getting signed with a top modeling agency. However, all is not lost. You can still find plenty of agencies that will sign you. With that scenario, it's best to go for agencies that aren't trying to specialize in runway modeling, but instead are looking for models for glamor shoots and ads. These types of agencies are more lenient on the age factor of most models, and they will also look at the entire package instead of just the height, weight, and age.

Get Yourself Ready for Open Calls

Before you go to an open call for any modeling agency, make an effort to look your best, no matter what your best may be. Remember, modeling agencies want to see a blank slate. They don't want a pre-made character. If you let them decide what angle they should try to market you with, the chances of you getting signed with that agency skyrockets.

To prepare yourself, you should first make sure that you are properly groomed. Look at what some of the models coming from that school are like, and emulate that. It is best to keep the unique features about yourself in the open, but don't become so unique that they have no idea what to do with you.

Be ready to show off some pictures. A decent headshot and a few pictures will help show them if you are perfect for their agency. Grab the best ones, and try to get a clear headshot that will show off your features. They will want to see how you will perform on camera.

Make sure your body is in shape. Remember, the sizes are ridged, so if you are on the edge of being a size 4, then wait a bit and try to tone yourself up so you are able to fit into their standards. It's better to be a size 0 or 2 than it is to be on the fringe like that.

Finally, go in with a winning attitude. You are going to get snobby people looking at you. These people only want the best, so make sure you know that. But, you don't need to be snobby back. If you just carry yourself with an air of confidence, and with a winning smile, then they will notice that. Confidence is sexy, and it will show them that you are not just a pretty face, but are able to show it on camera as well. Even if they say no, don't feel bad. Instead, just brush it off and try a different outlet. It's not the end of the world if you do this.

The most important thing to remember about top modeling agencies is that not everyone gets in, but if you play your cards right, you might be lucky enough to get a good representation at a well-known agency. These things take time; you will need to get yourself into the best condition possible when you go to your agency's open calls.

Chapter 3: Starting with Taking Care of Yourself

Being a top model is a dream of many women, but you cannot be a top model without taking care of yourself. Many women not only ruin their figures and their looks, but also ruin their lives by starving themselves into the proper sizes for modeling.

This is one of the worst things that you as a model can do to yourself. Starving causes acne, pallid skin, unsightly ribs, yellow teeth, and fatty deposits in unnatural areas. Does that sound attractive to you?

Thought not.

Eat Healthy Diet

The first step to taking care of yourself is to start eating the right food. Throw out all of the soda (diet sodas, too), candy, and other sugary foods from your pantry, and make a silent vow to stop ingesting all these toxic foods. Instead, opt for healthier snacks like pineapple, blueberries, beef jerky, and salads.

Fired food has a ton of fat and calories to it. It's also loaded with oils and salts, which can cause breakouts to happen. Fatty foods made with simple carbs instead of complex carbs are also another issue that has come into society as well. You need to get those foods out of your life, for they won't help you lose weight at all. Instead, eat foods that have complex carbs such as potatoes and meat.

After that, start learning the right portions. An actual serving of meat is only supposed to be about a deck of cards. Meanwhile a serving of mayonnaise is about the size of a poker chip. A serving of veggies is around the size of a baseball. It's important to look at the calories and serving sizes of meals, and if it's above the amount of calories you are supposed to take in each day, then work to make it less.

One of the main reasons many people are overweight is because they vastly underestimate the amount of calories they actually take in every day. What many don't realize, is that a 20,000 calorie diet is actually not what the average person should be having. Most of the time, people should have anywhere from 1300-1800 calories, depending on their lifestyle. If you are active, you will want more, but if you generally have a sedentary lifestyle, then you are going to need to cut back on it. Once you find out the real number, your pounds will drop rapidly, and your skin will look great.

Getting Into Shape

Basic hygiene is a must. Male or female, you will need white teeth, clear skin, and you will also need to smell nice. Otherwise, any go-see you will attend will not be fruitful. Many models pack a toothbrush, floss, and deodorant in their bags, too.

Make sure to get the dental care that you need. Teeth are becoming harder to manage as time goes on, and it is something that many have issues with. They don't take care of their teeth, and by the age of 20, many have to pay for expensive dental work. Make sure to brush twice a day and floss once a day. It is advisable to make sure that any cavities or other such things be taken care of immediately.

Proper dental hygiene is key in the modeling industry.

As for skin, make sure you visit a dermatologist if needed. Don't eat foods that cause breakouts. Lastly, you will need to exercise every day. Models need to be toned, because it shows up a lot better on film. This also is one of the key differences between a regular model and a top model. Most models work out with weights, pushups, curl ups, and add in a little bit of cardio and stretching. Hitting the gym with your friends will help you keep healthy and keep modeling for a longer time.

Chapter 4: Learn How To Pose

Posing for a photo isn't only a fun way to pass the day for models; it's the way that they put food on the table. This is the #1 skill that will make or break any model, and the hardest part about this skill is that everyone poses differently. In order to know what works well for you, you will need to start practicing.

The first step is to experiment, and it's the most important one. Stand in front of a full-length mirror and start doing poses. Just do whatever comes to your mind, and if you run out of ideas, look online. See what poses make you look bad, and what poses make you look awesome. Remember, not every pose works for every model. Some will give them an unseemly double chin, while other ones make the model look like a goddess. Just try them out, and see what is best for you.

If you are doing lingerie modeling, you should also try out different poses in lingerie.

People have different stomachs, and some of them show off the figure better than others. See which ones work for you, and make sure to pose yourself like that for pictures.

If you are still unsure of what works best, have someone take pictures of you to see what you like the most. There might be a few poses that just look terrible on camera, but you thought might be okay in the mirror. Have a friend that you trust take these pictures, and you can even judge them with the other person. Having a second set of eyes on the picture can do you a whole lot of good.

Before any shoot, take 5 to 15 minutes to practice poses in front of a mirror. Try standing poses, sitting poses, poses with props, and also poses where you are laying down. Don't only focus on how your body looks, either. Your face should be able to convey many different emotions as well. Try looking happy, sad, lost, bored, or even excited. Different photos will need different poses.

Work on making your eyes speak the words as well. Your facial expressions can do a whole lot, and sometimes the eyes can make a difference in the pictures. Try to work with the emotions and play around with them.

Soon you will be able to have a whole array of awesome expressions.

Next, it's time to start practicing your posing in front of a camera. Schedule some photo shoots with local photographers. This is called **TFP**, or **Time for Portfolio**.

TFP is something every model, new or veteran, needs to do every so often. You will need to network using the photographers you met through your TFP sessions, and you will also need the photos. Luckily, they need the photos as much as you do, so photographers will never charge for TFP. They may give you a few photos back, or they may give you a lot of photos back. It's advisable to not pester them about pictures either. That won't get them to you any sooner. TFP shoots are great as well if you are working on trying out new things because the worst thing that can happen is you find out that those shots aren't good for your portfolio.

One thing you have to be wary about, though, is the photographer. Make sure that you are working with honest ones, and not just guys that are trying to get you in bed. There are bad photographers out there who work in modeling only to get to women in a vulnerable position. You should meet up with the photographer and get to know him before a shoot. If it's a sexier one such as a lingerie shoot or even a nude shoot, bring a friend with you to have extra protection. Remember, doing this will allow you to have a better chance at being successful without compromising your own safety.

Once you have done a couple of photo shoots, it's time to actually look at the photos that you got. If you noticed that some photos look terrible because of your pose, avoid using that pose again. Also take a look and see if what you do compliments the rest of the outfit. A lot of models starting out don't realize that some of the poses they do don't work with certain outfits and such, and it's a flaw that needs to be seen before they do another shoot.

Most of the best poses will have your back arched, your shoulders squared, and your arms bent or rail straight. However, there are exceptions to this rule. Try to angle your face in ways that make you look flattering. Everyone can have the dreaded double chin in photos, even the ones with the most angular face. Try to see what angle your face works best, and learn to use that when you are modeling.

The important thing is to be imaginative with your poses.

Flipping through magazines will help you find poses, looks, and makeup ideas that you can use in your modeling career. Many models, once they are fresh out of ideas on how to pose, will start using yoga poses in photos.

Another great place to find poses is the Internet. There are thousands of pictures, and you can use them as ways to pose. Just type in "model poses" in the search engine, and you will be given a wide variety. Check out a few, maybe save them to your computer or phone, and try them out next time. That's the best way to go if you are not keen on spending money on magazines and need ideas fast. Also, typing in some famous models will give you pose ideas as well. Obviously, you won't look just like them, but it's great if you are out of ideas and need some inspiration in order to keep going.

Finally, you should also try to talk to friends or become acquaintances with fellow models. Sometimes photographers can help as well. Show them your pictures, and ask them how they feel about the pose. Just as a warning that it might be a bit rough on you. However, honest answers to this will help you out.

Asking for others to help can really extend your modeling repertoire. Remember, the people viewing you will be the ones ultimately judging the poses and the way the photo looks.

Of course, you won't know how a pose looks on you until you have actually done a shoot using it. So, start scheduling your first couple of time for portfolio shoots today!

Chapter 5: Learn to Network

If you wanted to be a model so that you wouldn't have to deal with people, you might want to reconsider that career choice. The only way top models get discovered is through networking. You need to know someone in the business in order to get business. Being a model is a very tough business to get into, so you will need to learn all of the tips and tricks to get you there. Networking is one of the best things to do in the world of modeling, for that allows new and amazing opportunities to open up for you, and with them you will be able to get farther into the business.

Whether the collaboration is with another model, a photographer, or even a hair and makeup stylist, you need to remember that networking is the key. This chapter will give you some ways to help you network with fellow models and other professionals in the industry. If you do this right, you will be able to become the best model ever.

- **Don't assume anything about anyone in the business.** That sloppily dressed person might be one of the most well-known movie producers in your area. That grossly overweight person might work with Elite Modeling agency. Many of the people in the business dress in an eccentric manner, and some designers may look like something out of a trippy modern art exhibit. Don't think any less of them because of the way they dress or the first impression they make. Just let them be, and you might realize that this person is way different than what you assume. Don't ever judge a book by its cover.

- **Do what you say you will.** The number one way to destroy your modeling career is to flake on a photo shoot. Don't flake, even if you are offered a paid shoot when you already had an unpaid shoot scheduled. If there is a problem with it, let the photographers and everyone else know in advance. At least give them a week's notice. If it's sudden, keep your commitments and just drop the other one or reschedule.

You may think that a paid shoot will get you father than an unpaid one. The truth is, it won't. There are tons of unpaid shoots that come about, along with tons of paid ones. If you flake out, that photographer or whoever it may be will never work with you again, and they will spread that like wildfire to their contacts. It's a sure way to get others to not want to work with you. There are thousands of models who look just like you, and will be happy to point out that you flake while they don't. So remember that before you are known as a no-show.

- **Be pleasant and polite with EVERY-ONE.** No one wants to work with a sour model. Being polite, pleasant, and easy to work with is a must in this industry. Believe it or not, many models who otherwise wouldn't get work manage to get paid work because of their personalities.

Even if the photographer is rude, it's better to be friendly than to be crass. Many models think that just because the photographer is being rude, it gives them a fair game to be rude back. Don't do that, for the photographer can destroy your reputation as well. Maybe they are having a bad day. Just get the shoot done, and then after that you can choose whether or not you want to work with that person ever again. It will make you still look great even in problematic circumstances.

- **Mention your skills, accomplishments, etc., everywhere you go.** People won't know much about you unless you tell them. Think of it as self-advertising, not boasting. This gets more models jobs than you'd ever believe.

- **Avoid drama.** This comes with being pleasant and polite with everyone, but since the fashion world is as catty as it gets, it's worth saying again. If someone starts drama with you, don't give into it. There are so many women who love to hate on other girls simply because they are in the business, and there might be some that are out to get you. Instead of being the person who gives into that sort of thing, just let the drama and names not bother you. Remember, in the modeling world, having a good attitude and work ethic will get you further than you might imagine.

Don't call people out on the wrongs that they have done to you until it's the right time. Say things in private, not in public. Don't post your drama on Facebook or other social media sites, because people you are networking with could see that, and they will definitely know what to think of you. Catfights, petty insults, and hissy fits will get you nowhere.

- **Be prepared for rejection, and don't take it personally.** Rejection isn't an easy thing to cope with, but it's one of the most commonly faced issues in the world of modeling. Try as hard as you can not to take it personally, and just smile and say "Thank You," instead. Remember that it's not the end of the world if you get rejected once. Just keep going and have a good time doing it. Take it as a life lesson, instead of a rejection that will only bring you down.

Chapter 6: Go For The High Profile Jobs

Money is a beautiful thing, but in the modeling industry, fame trumps money. Once you reach a certain level of notoriety, money will follow. Many new models make the mistake of focusing on paid jobs, which is something that you should never do unless you don't have any other job aside from modeling. (Even then, it's a very bad idea.)

Paid jobs are very hard for first-time models to get into. The people you want to work with may not realize the potential that you have. If you have no references of portfolio to give to them, you are going to be declined almost instantly.

Finding high profile jobs and getting them is what you need to do in order to become a top model. You need the right people to see your face, and you need to be able to show that you did some impressive modeling jobs on TV, on the news, etc. It's also important that you network and work with the right people. You have to have the look that they want, and you want to have the personality to go with it. If you do it right, you will get the gigs.

The better the jobs that you get, the more likely it is that someone big will spot you, and will ask you to sign with their agency. To get these, you just have to model. They are very hit and miss, and it's not always consistent. Sally might get a job modeling for Abercrombie and Fitch, but Sarah might not because she is a couple inches taller, or her eyes are too big. These little nuances are different factors that create the competition in these jobs.

The following are considered high profile jobs in the modeling industry:

- Runway (both high fashion, and regular swimsuit)
- Hair and makeup modeling for well-known hair artists
- ANY television appearances
- ANY magazine appearances
- Doing work with a major brand, such as Abercrombie and Fitch, Vogue, Gucci, and Chanel.

Try your hardest to shoot for these kinds of jobs.

Don't Be Scammed

If you hear about a high profile job, make sure that it isn't a fake modeling job. Fake modeling jobs are jobs that are not only unpaid; they will ask you to pay a fee in order to model for their line. These often come in the forms of showcases, beauty pageants, and similar options.

If you hear the words "Pay us," then run.

Not sure if it's high profile or a fake high profile job? Look for these signs.

- They ask you for money.
- It involves musicians you have never heard of.
- The advertisement insists that all of the biggest people in the modeling industry will be there, but you will need to pay an entry fee.
- It's a beauty pageant.
- Something seems oddly unprofessional about the behavior of the people running the show.

- The big one: SOMETHING JUST SEEMS WRONG!

Modeling high-profile jobs is hard. There is a lot of competition, and you need to be wary of the scammers out there. By doing this, you will ascend up the ranks to become a better model.

Chapter 7: Putting Together Your Portfolio

Deciding what kind of model you want to be will decide what your portfolio will look like. Since you have already begun your modeling career with TFP shoots, it's time to start sifting through photos to decide which ones are your best photos for your modeling genre.

Remember to try to emulate the top models in whatever genre that you choose to go into. For instance, plus size models should try to become the next Crystal Renn. High fashion models need to try to emulate supermodels like Tyra Banks. Glamour models should try to create a Pamela Lee type of appeal to their port.

When choosing pictures, don't let it be a crazy hodgepodge of stuff that doesn't work together. Pick pictures that work well and complement each other. Look for pictures that help enhance your best features, and scrap the ones that won't be right for your portfolio. There are definitely some guidelines that will help any portfolio become more hardy, more likely to get jobs, and more impressive to on-lookers.

When putting together your portfolio, consider the following rules.

- Pick your top 10 photos, and then your top 50. Your top 10 will be your "big sellers," for times when you can only submit one photo to fashion industry officials.

- Get a wide variety of different shots within a particular genre. You want to prove to clients that you can look amazing in a wide variety of colors, clothing, and makeup styles. Fashion models should consider having at least one formal shot, one casual shot, a head shot, and a 3/4 shot.

- If you aren't into glamour modeling, tone down on the flirtatious sides of your portfolio. You don't sell products and makeup with a pout and scanty clothing.

- Keep your photos as G-rated as possible while offering an edgy look to them. High amounts of emotion, commercial poses, and approachable attitudes conveyed through photos are more likely to get jobs than not. Sexy bodies are great, and if you are doing bikini modeling, it might be a great thing to have. However, if every single picture is something sexy or scandalous, it's not going to appeal to people.

- Don't be afraid to ask others what they think should be in your portfolio. More often than not, others can see the flaws in photos that you overlook. Get an impartial friend to help you pick your best ones. Better still, ask a fashion industry insider what their opinion on the matter happens to be.

- Models who are considering capitalizing off of parts would be wise to include close ups of their hands and feet in their portfolio. If you have a specific feature that you want to convey to others, such as your smile or your eyes, then pick photos that show those off. People who look at your portfolio are looking for parts of your body that can be used to sell products. If you have a picture that lights up your eyes and makes them look amazing, then that's definitely a picture that you should put in your portfolio.

Your portfolio is what gets you jobs, along with your references. If you don't have a good portfolio, continue to pursue TFP sessions until you have achieved a reasonable port. It's perfectly alright to admit to photographers that you aren't satisfied with your portfolio and want to improve it. Usually, that's the way to get the help that you need.

Chapter 8: Learn Your Safety Precautions!

Before you get serious in the modeling world, it's important to know how to keep safe in an industry that is often plagued with so-called photographers who don't have your best interests in mind.

There have been cases where up-and-coming models have disappeared from sight because of a lack of safety precautions. So, before you go to any major shoot (especially far from home), make sure to remember these safety tips.

- Always bring an escort. Many photographers refuse to shoot models who have escorts, however, because of the many dangerous situations that models have been caught in, it's a must. If a photographer isn't willing to let a friend accompany you to the shoot, then cancel the shoot.

- Talk to the photographer on the phone before you go. Otherwise, you might be in for a nasty surprise, or a flake.

- Ask your photographer for references. If a photographer can't find models who have had good experiences with him, chances are that this is because of some very serious issues. References can save lives, and they can also save a lot of time.

- Tell someone where you are going, and when you expect to be back. There have been cases where models who could have been saved could no longer be found because they never told anyone where they were going. By the time the models were found, it was too late.

- If you think something doesn't feel right, you are right. Cancel the shoot.

- Don't be afraid to say "NO!" If something is beyond your liking or your limits, then you shouldn't have to do it.

The main reason why many models let their bad experiences ride is because they worry that their reputation will be marred because of their honesty about a photographer. Think of it this way - would you rather cancel a shoot and stay safe, or would you rather get hurt and stay quiet?

Chapter 9: Getting Signed

Getting signed with an agency is a feat that should be attempted only after several months of modeling as a freelancer. Models should only look for legitimate modeling agencies, with a real modeling agency license number. Otherwise, they may end up on the wrong side of a bad deal.

Getting signed is basically the mark of a real model, and one of the biggest steps to becoming a top model. This is because agencies deal with only the best models in the industry, and only will work with models that they know can be in demand.

There are several things to do that can boost your chances of getting signed with an agency. Model calls are how agencies find their next models.

How to be Successful in Model Calls

First, get your hair, nails, eyebrows, and skin perfected. Wear light (NATURAL) makeup, and keep your clothing as casual and "blank slate" as possible when you go to your first model call. Don't wear jewelry, or anything that can detract from your natural look.

Next, have a good attitude. The easiest way to guarantee that you will not make it in the modeling world is if you throw a tantrum when an agency rejects you. And believe me, agencies have rejected supermodels before. Instead of shouting at the agents, crying, or anything of that level, smile and say thank you. Then, go outside to collect yourself.

Manners are crucial in this area of the modeling world. Say "please," "thank you," and "you're welcome" as much as you can. Smile placidly, and let people see that you have grace under pressure. Agents love a calm, happy model. They detest divas.

If you get a consultation, talk like a businessperson. Explain that you understand that modeling is an industry, not a hobby. Also explain that you will allow them to market you as they see fit, and that you are willing to go to go-sees.

Don't make any demands. Talk about your experience, your capabilities, and any related training that will make you a more marketable model.

With hope and perseverance, you will get signed.

Chapter 10: Going To Go-Sees

If you haven't been to a model meet where photographers and designers decide whether or not you actually fit the role, you haven't been to a go-see yet. Go-sees are exactly what they sound like. You go there so that they can actually see you to make sure who you are. They are a common find in many agencies, and also are very important when it comes to major gigs.

When you go to a go-see, you have to expect certain things. For one thing, you have to expect rejection, but hope for acceptance by the fashionistas. You also have to expect that the people who are running the show expect you to look polished, good as new, and totally refreshed. The fact is that go-sees are often very stressful, and require a lot of effort to prepare for. However, shows which have go-sees are often the shows which are worth attending. They are often high-profile or well-paid jobs. Therefore, it's worth going to a go-see to have a chance at it.

Going to a go-see means that you need to put in the same effort that you would in order to go to a paid shoot. You need to have makeup on, your nails immaculate, your hair coiffed, and your clothes fresh. Sloppiness is a cardinal sin in the world of modeling, and during go-sees, sloppiness will cause people to refuse to hire you later on.

Next, it's important that you actually show up if you agree to show up. If you do decide to show up, make sure that you are on time. Don't arrive late! Flakes and lateness are highly frowned upon, even during go-sees. Keeping your hand on time and arriving early are the most important ways to keep your chances at modeling high. After all, the most beautiful girl in the world won't get hired for a runway show if she doesn't show up to the go-see. On the other hand, an average girl will get hired if she is the only one who actually attends.

Chapter 11: Branching Out

One of the worst things that can happen to a model is for her to become pigeonholed. You want to be able to be considered for all sorts of different jobs, not only jobs in one genre. Sadly, many young models believe that they are doing themselves a favor by pre-typecasting themselves before they even get to watch their modeling careers blossom.

In order to allow yourself branching out into different genres (and therefore proving your versatility to agents), follow these simple but useful rules.

- Keep your portfolio as varied as possible. Have high fashion, a commercial shot, a bikini shot, and even an extreme alternative shot in your portfolio. Your goal with your portfolio should be diversity. So, try to look as different as possible from shot to shot.

- Attend different modeling events, and try to market yourself to different audiences. Try art modeling with painters, high fashion runway with designers, and parts modeling with jewelry makers. Part of your versatility should be your ability to work with many different people without having to worry.

- If you have any tattoos, you are probably already typecast. If you don't have any tattoos, don't even think about getting ink done. Tattoos are the #1 limiting factor when it comes to models' careers. Don't do this to your modeling career. Stay as tattoo-free as possible.

- When going to your next agency meeting, go-see, or even get together with industry professionals, dress as nondescript as possible. Let yourself be the blank canvas that people want to see. Give your possible employers the chance to paint you a personality that they would want to shoot. Believe it or not, this is one of the easiest ways to avoid getting stuck to one genre.

- Emphasize that you are not just a glamour model, or just a fashion model. Make an effort to tell photographers, designers, and more that you are an all-around model with a specialization in one specific field. The more that you tell them you want to branch out, the more that they will listen and let you branch out.

Chapter 12: Improve Yourself

No top model, no matter how genetically gifted she or he may be, ever becomes a top model without trying to improve herself as a person, and as a model. This industry is extremely fluid, and no one is the same person that they were a year ago. In order to be able to stay a "fresh face" in this industry, you will have to keep pushing towards a better you.

Why? Because everyone else is working on being able to be the best model they can be. If you notice that the body type that is in Vogue changed, then try a new workout routine that will help tone your muscles in that manner. If you noticed that blondes are now getting more work than redheads, consider going for a lighter shade. Update your look frequently, and make sure that the look you are working with actually is worth the upkeep that you have to do in order to maintain it.

The best way to improve yourself in posing is to ask a trusted photographer friend for their opinions on how you should pose. Style and makeup should be the realm of your most trusted stylist. If you are signed with an agency, make an effort to consult with them about how you can improve your marketability. They will be able to provide plenty of great advice, and your agents will also be very glad to have hired you after all that.

Of course, the most important kind of improvement involves your outlook on life. Let both the good and the bad experiences you have as a model illuminate your ideas on life. The world of modeling offers everyone a lot of experiences which can help you become a better person, both professionally and socially. Instead of using your bad experiences as a way to learn about yourself, and use what you learn to improve yourself.

Having a career as a model means that you will never really be able to take a break from self-improvement. You are always going to be working on getting better jobs, and you will always find something new about yourself. Perhaps, that's the real beauty about being a real model.

Chapter 13: The Power of Social Media

Social media can be a great networking tool, and as a model starting out, it's advisable to have a social media account for it. Social media is one of the best things out there if used wisely. It can also turn into one of the worst things if you are not careful. This chapter will go over the power of social media, the best ones to have, what to post, and what to avoid.

Why Social Media?

Social media is a great way to get more reach. It allows more people to network with you, and is a surefire way to get noticed. Social media is one of the most widely used mediums of communication in the world today. Nearly everyone has a Facebook account, and many people have more than one social media account. You can also have other means of contact on there as well. Even though you might not get jobs directly from it, you will be able to draw in a bigger crowd in order to help you go further in your modeling career.

There are tons of models that have a Facebook page or a Twitter account, so you can network with them there. You can work on collaborations, and many photographers are on there as well. Some of the photographers might just be hobbyists or have other intentions, so it's important to look at their work before you agree to work with one. As for the models, you will be able to connect with more women and men out there, and you can even plan meet-ups where you shoot together, or they might refer you to other people. It's a simple way to get your name out.

Social media is also great for photographers, modeling agents, and potential clients to see what you are like and what you have to offer. If you have a page, you can post the best content there for them to see. They can determine how good you are at what you do, and if you are worth working with.

Which Is Best?

You might wonder which social site is best. Each one has its own pros and cons. You can have all, or maybe just one to help with your modeling career. Here are some of the major sites and their pros and cons.

- **Twitter**: as you might know, twitter is a site that allows you to post "tweets" about various things. Whether they are status updates, funny photos and videos, or even incentives to go to a site, it's a great means to get the message out quickly. There are some limitations with it though. You have to say everything in 140 characters or less. You can't use more, because tweets are supposed to be short and sweet. But, if you have a quick message about something and want to show it off, then that's the way to go.

  Another problem with Twitter is that there is a limit to how many tweets you can send per day. If you want to network with someone, and you are tweeting with them back and forth, they will lock up your account after a certain number of tweets. It might temporarily stop you from continuing to market yourself, so be careful when you use it.

Most models have Twitter accounts, but the issue with so many famous ones is that they rarely respond to Twitter tweets. You might have to send them a private message in order to talk to them. But, if you are trying to get to high-profile modeling, you are going to have a very hard time getting in touch with any model, for they get sent thousands of tweets each day.

One of the benefits of Twitter is that you can post links to content, so if you have a site, it'll get more interest in the landing page. This is great for models who want to sell prints in order to gain side income. Also NSFW (Not suitable/safe for work) content is allowed on Twitter, so if you have either sexy or nude shoots, then you can link them to the site in order to gain further reach.

- **Facebook**: Facebook is usually the first media site that everyone thinks about when the word social media comes to their mind. Facebook is the most popular, and nearly everyone has an account. It's a great way for a model to market herself, but like other social media sites, there are pros and cons to it.

The biggest pro about Facebook is the number of people you are able to reach. You will be able to have more people check you out, and more people will want to collaborate with you. Just like with Twitter, there are also many modeling pages. You can promote yourself and learn to network with other models and photographers. The messaging system for Facebook pages is great. It will allow you to have more reach when it comes to the various people that you are itching to promote to. Facebook also lets you have your pictures there. You can organize them into folders. It will allow you to keep a neat portfolio there for people you are networking with to check out.

Now comes to the cons of using Facebook. The biggest one is that Facebook has a silly algorithm that they use to calculate reach. Between 1 and 10,000 likes, your reach is about 10% of the people. If you are shared on other outlets and such, it can turn into more. But past 10,000 likes, they are only allowing 1% of the people to see what you are doing. You can "get notifications" to have more people see it, but the problem is, most of your viewers don't do that. Therefore, they might not see your posts sometimes, and if you have important announcements it might be hard to get full coverage. Facebook does allow you to reach more than 10% of the people, but of course it requires that you pay for the promotion.

Another con is that it doesn't allow NSFW content. It allows you to post some of the sexier stuff, and usually lingerie and swimsuit modeling is fine. But implied nudes and nude modeling are usually not able to stay up unless heavily censored. They might even get you if there is underbust in the picture as well, so if you are a model that does NSFW content, it's not advisable to use Facebook to market that.

Then there is the con of the people. Sometimes you will pull in fans that like to make sexual comments towards you. Some models have been able to tell them to knock it off. Usually this happens to models that post a lot of sexy pictures, so if you are the type of model that usually does sexier things, be prepared for the comments and offensive messages from people.

Sometimes people will judge you based off your Facebook page, so it's important to know that you are being judged by people based off of what you post. It's not smart to have content on your Facebook that could cause potential people to deviate from working with you. If you post photos of you drinking or doing drugs, people won't want to be around that. If you are going to post on social media, make sure it's clean.

- **Instagram**: This is a newer social media site and great for pictures. With Instagram, you will gain followers; and unlike Facebook, there is no algorithm that goes along with this, so all your followers will see the posts. It's a great site if you want to showcase your modeling.

The biggest pro is the reach. Everyone sees it, and you can build up quite a following with this site. People will look at your work, and they will be interested. NSFW content can be posted on Instagram. It's a more lenient site, so as long as you tell your viewers beforehand, you will be able to post it.

The cons are the fact that they might compress the picture and crop out important things. If that's the case, you can get apps from your smartphone store to help fix that. Usually it's a simple fix, but you will have to go through every photo you want to post with the app in order to prevent it from being cropped out.

- **Tumblr**: If you are a model who wants to have a blog, then Tumblr is for you. With a blog you can tell people about upcoming things, and you can also gain more reach. Tumblr blogs are great for those who want to have a following in another corner of the social media community, and it works well.

You can customize your Tumblr blog to a great extent, and you can choose your own designs for it. You will be able to have a profile picture, along with a cool background to it. You can post pretty much whatever you want on it. Tumblr is much more lenient than other social media sites, so if you have adult content, you can post it there without getting banned or reported by people. Tumblr is great for those who want to have a site where they can post whatever they want, and it's one that is simple to use and easy to get benefits out of.

The issue with Tumblr, though, is the drama. Tumblr is the center of major drama, regardless of what niche you are in. There are anonymous people who are going to hate you just for hating purposes. But there are also a lot of supporters too. Many of the haters love to start drama, and they can harass you constantly. If you are going to use Tumblr, make sure that you have a strong spine, for many of the people on there don't have a filter or know how to say nice things. Just be ready for the anonymous hate, which is probably one of the biggest issues with Tumblr.

- **Model Mayhem**: Model Mayhem is a site that is actually for models. It's a place where you can post your portfolio in order to get some work. You will be able to network with other people, and it's the best social media site to help forward your modeling career. There, you can talk about all the types of modeling you want to do. You can even apply for casting calls, talk to other photographers and models, and ascend to a new level of modeling by using that. There is everything from TFP gigs to high-profile jobs. It's perfect for those who want to get a good foot into the modeling door.

There are tons of casting calls you can find on Model Mayhem that range from local gigs to those that are all over the place. You can have artistic nudes up there as well as normal content. It's great if you want to build an online portfolio to market to other sites.

There are a few cons with Model Mayhem. You can put up to 15 photos up at no cost. If you want more you will have to pay a fee. This fee isn't that much, but if you are not serious about using this, it can be a waste of money. Then there is the problem of spammers. There are some accounts on there that are there solely to spam you with different things. At some point you will probably get hit with these fake photo shoots and gigs. Don't fall for it. If you suspect that it's a spam, don't even bother to open it. Instead, delete it and move on. If you do open it, the spammers will then continue, and at one point, they could even ghost your account. You can talk to the admins of the site, who are super helpful, to get your profile back, but it's a whole bunch of unnecessary work that you don't need to do. It's better to be safe than sorry, so watch out for that.

What to Post

There are certain things that you should post on your social media sites to help you generate a larger audience and create a bigger following.

- **Pictures**: Make sure to give photographer credit first before you posting pictures, as that could end up being a big issue later on. You also need to have the best images up there. Uploading sub-standard images would communicate the wrong thing to many people. Instead, put your best foot forward and make sure that everything is copyrighted, watermarked, and kept track of.

- **Posts about Life**: You can post what's going on with your life to keep everyone up to date on various things. You don't need to tell them everything under the sun, but a bit of information on what you are doing and what plans you have. You can also make posts to interact with fans, and that will get your reach up.

- **Cool Skills/Special Talent**: One of the best things to post on social media sites is the cool skills or special talent you have. This is a surefire way to get your reach up. Potential people whom you may want to work with will be interested. For example, if you are insanely good at makeup, then make sure you post this. You can post how-to's, tutorials, or just basic information on this subject. It will not only generate interest, but also can showcase your work.

- **Links to Your Site**: If you have a personal modeling site, you can link it from social media sites. It's a great way to boost traffic to your own site, as links will be given preference to other sorts of posts.

What NOT to Post

There are things that you shouldn't post on social media. These are just as important as the things you should post. Posting the right things will get you reach, while posting things that don't help will cripple you. Some of the people who view your page might be determining whether or not to work with you, and it's one of the things that you should be wary about. Make sure to not have the following on your page, for they could cause your modeling career to go down the drain.

- **Drama**: The one thing you should never post on social media sites is drama. Drama is everywhere, and it seems like the modeling world is full of it along with any other place. Drama can get very catty, as many women like to intimidate others in order to cause them to fall. It'll probably annoy you, but it's best to just not give into that. Don't let them get to you, and it'll make your life all the easier.

- **Personal Info**: The last thing you should be doing is giving out too much information. Some of the people viewing your page might have unsavory intentions. They might be thinking that it's okay to stalk you, but obviously that isn't the case. You should protect yourself and never give out personal information on a social media site. If you do that, you will be able to have a safer and better experience.

- **Inappropriate Content**: Nudity can be okay on some platforms, but not on others. Drug abuse and drinking are also inappropriate. Many people post pictures of themselves partying, and they get tagged in pictures where they were doing drugs. Not only is that bad to have on a profile period, it's even worse to have on social media. You don't want to be judged by those pictures, so it's best to not have those on there. Make sure that you check everything before you post.

- **Unimportant/Irrelevant Things**: Nobody really cares about the fact that you say the sky is blue, and posts that are boring won't get the reach that you are trying to get. Just keep things strictly modeling, and you will be fine.

- **Unflattering Pictures**: Unflattering pictures will stand out more than the flattering ones. Make sure that the pictures enhance you instead of making you look worse. You can laugh at bad pictures in private, but don't put them out there for the entire world to see.

Chapter 14: Makeup Techniques for Success

With modeling, there is another side to the game that you need to work on. That's the world of makeup. If you are not proficient with it, you will have issues getting gigs. Many times, there might not be a makeup artist for TFP shoots, so you are on your own when it comes to getting yourself ready. This chapter will go over the different styles you can use, along with tips and techniques to make yourself look amazing.

Styles for Success

Makeup can make or break a model. It will enhance your emotions, and allows you to communicate what you want through your expressions. You need to know some of the styles that help you to be successful.

- **Business Style**: This is a great style for those who are going to casting calls, or if you are at a shoot that requires you to have just the basics. What you will need is some foundation, an eye shadow that matches your skin tone, some primer, mascara, eyeliner, blush, and lipstick. You will also need concealer if you have blemishes that can't be hidden with the foundation.

  To start, you can use foundation to help even out the skin. Then, you will give your eyes a touch of eye shadow. Don't put on too much. Just graze it over the lid. After that, add in some eyeliner around the edges of your eyes. Again, don't use too much, but try to get the bottom of the eye and the side of it. Then, add a tinge of mascara to it. After that, add blush to ghost over your cheeks. Then, put on the lipstick or lipgloss. Just have it a little bit over your lips, and it will make all the difference.

- **A Wilder Look**: This is for shoots or gigs that demand you to have a bigger and crazier set of eyes. To do this, get a crazy eye shadow color. Make sure it goes with the outfit, so that it doesn't clash. For example, if you have a blue dress, a shimmering blue eye shadow works.

First, use the concealer and foundation to help clean up your face. Then use primer to enhance your eyes. After that, put the eye shadow on, blending it in. You can use darker eye shadow to help enhance it as well. At the end of it, you will add in the mascara to help make your eyes pop. Do it over the entire bottom of the eye and then over half of the top part of the eye. It will make your eyes look wilder and pop out more. For the blush, just ghost it over your cheeks. If you want to, you can use a wild lipstick, but most of the time it's best if you keep the wilder stuff at a minimum in that area.

- **Making Your Face Look Longer**: Many times, models have to make their faces look longer. They want to have a more angular jaw, and it will help with the double chin issues. The best way to contour is to get the right makeup, but you can also use just regular makeup for this. Ben Nye is a great brand for those who want to have a better-looking face that also screams beauty.

To do this, you put foundation and concealer on. Then, take an eye shadow that is darker than your skin tone and put it against your jaw line, starting from your ear. You can also put a darker eye shadow under your eyes to help eliminate under-eye circles and make you look better. You then blend it in, making it look clean. After that, you can apply a darker eye shadow at the top in order to help create more shadow and make your eyes pop out. You can use mascara and eyeliner to make your eyes stand out too.

Tips for Makeup

Here are tips that will help make your makeup look even better. Most of the time you will have a stylist on bigger shoots, but if you are just doing work to help promote yourself, it's best that you know what to do and what not to do.

- **Make sure you know what's best for you.** The biggest thing models seem to forget is that not every style works on everyone. They will believe that it's just a good idea, when in reality the style looks terrible on them. You should try out different styles, but then see what's best for you.

- **Invest in good makeup supplies.** You need to have professional makeup to look better. The materials are expensive, but it's worth it. To start, you should just get a good makeup palette. Then work from there to get the best stuff that you can. It's important to have proper makeup, for it will help enhance your modeling and take it to a whole new level.

- **Learn new techniques.** The Internet is a great place to learn new techniques. You can learn how to do various things just from watching YouTube videos. It's an important skill in this line of work, and it's one that you should look into.

- **Use colors that complement you.** Colors that complement you will help you look more amazing than before. Some colors just look tacky on certain skins. If you use the wrong one, it will create a bad image in the picture. You should see what works best, and try not to go too crazy on the shades and hues of each of the various makeup tools.

- **Don't get too heavy with it.** Heavy makeup may look good in some cases, but most of the time it looks cheesy, and you can end up looking like a drag queen. Makeup is essential for pictures, mainly because if you don't have it the camera washes out your face. However, don't go too crazy with it. Instead, try to use enough so that you will make an impression with the photo, but not so much so that it makes you look like a cheap hooker. Moderation is key with makeup.

- **Use fake eyelashes.** Fake eyelashes will help make your eyes stand out. If you have eyes that aren't big, then it's important that you make sure to help complement them using fake eyelashes.

You can get these for cheap. They are going to hurt when you take them off, but they give you fuller eyes and help you look better.

- **Eliminate under-eye circles.** One of the biggest problems people have is under-eye circles. This can happen due to lack of sleep or when there is too much fluid buildup in your eye area. It drapes over into pockets, and with them you will have eyes that look tired and worn out. To fix this, you should get some under-eye cream and use makeup under the eyes to get rid of it. Usually a dark eye shadow will do the trick. This will save your photographer quite a headache when he is trying to edit your photos, for it's a problem that takes a lot of skill to remedy.

- **Don't be afraid to get out of your com-fort zone.** Let's face it, sometimes being introduced to the world of makeup and trying new things can scare you. Many don't know what the best look will be until they try it. Many times you will look at yourself in the mirror and feel like it's unreal. If you actually try out different makeup tips and tricks, you will be able to learn different techniques, and you can work on enhancing them as well. Makeup isn't something that stays stagnant all the time. It will change with due course.

Makeup is a fun thing to learn, and it's important when it comes to modeling. Everyone is different, so make sure that you are able to change things up and go the right course. Remember that even if you have issues at the onset, you will learn from it and have a better time later on.

Chapter 15: Hair Tips for Success

Hair is an interesting part of the body to work with. Many don't know how to convey the best styles out there or how to style to make it look good. Similar to makeup, hair is crucial to modeling. You will eventually have hair stylists that will do your hair, but you have to learn at the onset what hair styles suit you best. You might also want to try out different things. Hair is just as important as clothes in modeling, so it's important to keep it up.

Tips to Awesome Hair

Here are some tips to help make your hair styles pop out, especially in photos and casting calls.

- **Make sure your hair is fully dyed.** Dyed hair can look great, and in some photos it really stands out. But if you don't keep up with it, your roots will show and it will look bad. Red color typically lasts the shortest, so make sure to get more hair dye if you have red hair. Black lasts the longest, and if you are going from a bright color to black, it will stay in for a few months. If you see your roots starting to show, you need to touch them up. It's also advisable that you don't use developer that's too high, for it'll fry your hair. You should also ensure that the hair dye you get isn't box dye, for the developer isn't as strong and it won't last as along.

- **Don't go for wild colors unless needed.** Wild colors might seem like a good idea in theory, but instead it will make your hair look bad. Wild colors will scream unprofessionalism unless you are going into alternative modeling, or if the person you are shooting with wants that. Don't ever go to an open call or a potential gig with hair that looks like something out of a Goth club. Instead, keep it in professional colors.

- **Get rid of oil.** Oily hair is one of the biggest problems that many people have. It is obvious and hard to manage. Try to use shampoos that will help get rid of oil, and work to not use too much shampoo and conditioner. By doing so, you will have hair that looks great and doesn't have excess amount of oil in it.

- **Keep it in a professional hairdo.** Don't go for the crazy styles such as shaved heads or anything like that. When you are up for a casting call, keep it in a professional look. You can keep it straight, curly, or with a bit of wave to it. You will want to look your best, for it will show itself to the people you could be working with. The crazy hair styles might come around if you have a gig that calls for them, but try to keep the hair as professional as possible.

- **Give a bit of a unique feeling to it.** Even though you want to be professional, give yourself a bit of uniqueness. Straight and boring hair might be okay to a few people, but most people you will be working with will want hair that can be styled in interesting ways. Maybe try wearing it in buns or cute little updos. It's a good way to keep yourself looking great, and the people you are trying to impress will notice.

- **Keep it clean.** To be a model you have to have a good sense of cleanliness. You want to have a nice-looking body that is both bathed and groomed. You also have to have hair that looks great, and even has a shine to it. Hair that looks clean and healthy will impress people, for it will show that it can take different styles. If your hair is having trouble, try to get different products that will help make your hair better. Try to stay clear of too many chemicals if you need to rejuvenate the hair. If you are a person who's dyed their hair a lot, it might be best to just give life back to it instead of trying to put as many products as you can into it.

- **Avoid hair gel.** Hair gel might look cool in some cases, but in general it doesn't hold well. If you are trying to style your hair into a quirky way, it's best to use styling glue or freeze spray to hold it. It will hold for hours and on-ly come off when you wash it out. This way, you can keep the style that you want, and you can even mold it to im-prove the way it is.

Chapter 16: Dress for Success

The world of modeling requires that you dress right. You need to look good, or else people won't' give you the time of day. The following tips will help ensure that you are looking your best for that casting call.

- **Don't wear grungy clothes.** Remember, you have to be a professional when it comes to modeling. There are thousands of others trying to make it, and some might think that they are better than you. The way to beat them is with a professional attitude, and dressing professionally goes along with it. Wear clothes that you would wear to a job interview. It will show that you are serious and also convey that you are able to handle a job like this. Don't be in jeans and a t-shirt unless you are supposed to.

- **Wear colors that make you look good.** Wearing colors that enhance your beauty will definitely win over others. If you are going to an open call, or to any meet-up, a nice dress can always make you stand out. If you wear crazy clothing that doesn't work with you, people are not going to take you seriously. You will want to have a good image, so try to find a nice dress that looks professional and complements your beauty. It is okay to step a bit out of your comfort zone, but don't go so far as wearing patterns that look terrible on you.

- **If you are bigger, avoid horizontal stripes.** For people who are plus size, wearing horizontal stripes will make you look even bigger. Remember, you are trying to make yourself look more flattering, not less. Find clothes that have vertical stripes to them, as vertical stripes will enhance your beauty and make you look taller.

- **Look in the mirror before leaving.** Before you leave to go to any gig, take a couple minutes and look over yourself. Check over everything to make sure that it looks great, and you will be happy with the results. If there is something amiss, it's best to fix it right then and there. If there are stray hairs on your body, take them off. If you see something is dirty, clean it up. If you think you are showing too much skin, try to think of ways to limit it, either that or don't wear that dress at all.

- **Don't dress sexy.** A sexy outfit is nice to wear when you are going out and partying, but in a modeling sense, dressing too revealing will hurt your reputation. Some people you might work with might not like sexier stuff, and they might be gravitating towards ideas that aren't that. If you show up in a sexy miniskirt and a low-cut top, first not only will it look bad because it's unprofessional, but it will also seem like you are trying to do something else besides landing a modeling gig. Remember, this is like any other job interview, and if you are dressing like that at a normal interview, you will not get the job.

- **Pair clothes with accessories.** Fashion has a key role in the world of modeling, so you have to have some sense of it. You should know how to pair outfits together, because not only will you look better, it will show the people who are looking at you that you know how to coordinate yourself. In the beginning, you might be the one providing the photos with your own personal flair to it. You need to be unique, and a unique accessory will show that you are not just one of those people who would wear any old thing, but instead you are a person who has an inkling of understanding of what they are doing, along with determination to make things work.

Clothing is a big part in the world of modeling. You have to know how to dress the part. Don't be afraid to experiment, but make sure that you have the right outfit when it comes to getting ready for a big shoot. You will notice how important the use of clothing can be in a modeling interview. With the right clothing, you will be able to get more gigs.

Chapter 17: How to Walk the Walk

To be a top model, you have to know how to walk and compose yourself. It will show that you are able to hold yourself up, especially if you are going into runway modeling. This chapter will go over the basics of how to walk the walk, and how to have a modeling walk that will not only ooze confidence, but will also breathe success.

The first thing you have to do is remember to be confident. Even if you normally are not, pretending to at least have a slight air of confidence will make a difference. People will see that, and many of them don't really care about much else. They want a confident boy or girl to flock the stage. Confidence is key, and if you have that, the rest is easy.

When walking, you should keep yourself straight up. Don't slouch. Slouch is a typical habit that many people have. It looks tacky when you walk that way. You need to keep your back straight, but not so straight that you look like a doll. You should also make sure that your head is up -- that's a sign of confidence. Also, don't sit into your hip unless the pose calls for that. It's not a good thing to do, and it puts undue stress on your legs.

When walking, it's best to lead with your right foot. This will show that you have a dominant walk. Then just put one foot in front of the other with toes facing forwards.

When you are walking, don't have your arms stiff. A big thing that some models do that looks bad is they have a very stiff walk. They might have a great stride, but when they walk, their hands are fixed in one location and refuse to move. It's extremely distracting, and it makes you look like a robot. Have your hands loosely at the side, but not so loose that they look like spaghetti noodles. Try to keep your composure to make your strides look more professional.

Keep eye contact when you walk. Don't be afraid to look at the person you are doing the audition for. Just keep yourself looking at them. You can smile as well, but eye contact is the way to do this. If you are looking down or anywhere else, it not only makes you look lack of confidence, but also conveys that you don't want the job. Look at people, communicate to the audience using your eyes, and you will have a much more successful time when it comes to walking.

Another thing you have to watch out for is your mouth. Don't have it hanging open like a bump on a log. It will make you look dead, or that you are not paying attention. The person who's watching you might think that you are not skillful enough to hold your face in the right position.

Make sure that your shoulders don't rise. Shoulders that are tall and stiff are obvious, and it makes you not only look nervous, but it also makes your whole body stiff as a board. It also doesn't convey a confident image to the people you are auditioning for. Instead, walk with your shoulders down and your head up. Don't be afraid to practice pushing down your shoulders. Many people naturally walk with a bit of raised shoulders, but in the world of modeling, that is a big no-no.

Finally, it's important to practice. Practice walking at home. Do it from your bedroom to the kitchen when you want to get food. Do it from the bathroom to the front door. Just try walking like that. You can even do it at work.

You might get a few looks because of how confident you look, but it's a great way to get used to it. Watch your walk and see where you can improve. The best way to do that is to record yourself walking as you walk through various places. Look at the recording and you will notice what you need to fix in order to make yourself look better.

Walking might seem a simple little thing, but in the world of runway modeling, and even in regular modeling, it's imperative to have this down. Doing it right will allow you to have an air of confidence to yourself. And you will be able to convey that confidence to others.

Chapter 18: Must-Have Traits of a Top Model

To be a top model, you have to have a sort of approach to others that will make you look appealing. You need to have a personality that screams that others should work with you, and have the attitude that others want to deal with. This chapter will go over a few of the qualities that you need to have in order to be the next top model.

- **Friendly**: Being a friendly person gets you far in the world of modeling. Be nice to others. Have a friendly vibe. Clients and other models will appreciate it. Being friendly shows that you care about others and people will want to work with you more. Especially when you are in a catty place, being friendly can make you look even better.

- **Confident**: You can't let every single little thing get you down. So what if you are not the right model for a gig? It's not the end of the world. Just keep on going, and it will allow you to have better air to yourself. This trait is so important that I've dedicated the next chapter to discuss more about it.

- **Truthful**: A truthful model is a model that can be successful. You have to tell people the truth regarding what you can and can't do. You have to give them all of the facts, and you want to be honest with them. Being a truthful person will allow you to get more work, and people will know that you are a person with integrity. If there is something that you haven't done, let them know. Even if you are not experienced in it, you can get experience later on. It's better to be a truthful person that people can rely on than someone who isn't able to be used because she won't give you the straight answer.

- **Trusted**: This is part of truthfulness, but in a different way. You should be at your gigs when it's time, and if you can't make it, let them know as soon as possible. Things do happen, so it's better to be honest and try to convey the facts to people than to be an untrustworthy person that can't work efficiently. You should try to be there for people, for they are taking the time to be there for you.

- **Happy**: Being happy will get you far. Happiness is something that many models don't engage in. They always want to be in on the drama, or they want to have an air of sadness or anger to them. It's not a good thing, for people notice that. If you are happy when you are on the job, it will show. People will like to be around you, and you will have a much better time.

- **Undramatic**: Don't be a drama queen or king. Don't be a person who is known for the drama that they cause or get into. Whether you are famous or not, people will always have something to say. You should try to be the bigger person when conflicts come your way. Say goodbye to the drama, and work on making yourself into the best person that you can be.

- **Helpful**: Some models might come to you for help. You can give tips and advice. Just don't let them walk all over you. Modeling may be competitive, but you don't have to be seen as selfish in front of others. Try to help others when you can. It will come back to you when you need help one day.

- **Patient**: Probably one of the worst traits a model can have is being impatient. If you are a person who has a low threshold for patience, you are not going to go very far in the modeling world. Having a patient vibe to yourself will help you out, and you will be happier. You will be seen as someone who can wait, not as someone who is complaining all the time. Whiners never do well in this line of work.

- **Personable**: You want to be one of those people who has a good vibe to them. You want to be a person that others can rely on, and one that they can associate with. You want to be happy, friendly, and confident, and you also want to still maintain that atmosphere even when things go awry. You are not going to get every modeling gig under the sun, but you will be able to at least get a few over time. Continue to smile despite all the issues that you might have encountered.

- **Persistent**: Be a person who doesn't give up. The world of modeling doesn't have a place for quitters. Instead of being a person who throws a fit every time he or she is not given the job, just keep your emotions to yourself when you hear the news. You can go home and cry, but only do it for a few minutes. You can eat a bit of ice cream, and then get right back to it. Giving up is the pathway to failure as a model.

Modeling is probably one of the hardest career tracks to get into. However, if you keep these different traits in mind and work on them whenever possible, you will be successful, and it will make everything that you worked for worth it in the end.

Chapter 19: The Best Modeling Tip You'll Ever Learn

It's true that not just anyone can be the next Naomi Campbell or Tyra Banks, but it is possible for just about anyone to be taken seriously as a model.

The only way to establish yourself as a great model is by having the same thing that every major top model always has with her – **confidence**.

Confidence is what allows good models to become great.

Why?

Because when you are confident, you see all of the beauty, poise, and grace that you possess, and you flaunt it without having to go overboard to prove your point.

The fact is that a model that isn't confident is going to be unable to really pose as well as she could. Every smile that a model with low esteem shows on camera will appear faked, strained, and very odd.

A lack of confidence causes every pose that a model strikes to look strained, tired, or scared. People pick up on this and often will refuse to shoot with a model once this happens.

There have been many cases where an undermined confidence in a model has caused a career failure, or a failure to launch a career in the fashion industry.

How to Keep Your Self Confidence High

Modeling is a fun activity, but the modeling industry is famous for cutting people down verbally, and also giving people a much-needed reality check.

Keeping your confidence high as a model is critical, but it is also a very difficult feat for anyone to do continually. In order to keep your self-esteem intact, it's important to follow several rules.

- Don't hang out with people who undermine you confidence in yourself. They might say that their negative comments are "just jokes," or that they are "just pointing out the truth," but the bottom line is that it's negativity that you don't need.

You don't need people who don't believe in you, and you definitely don't need people who are putting you down instead of supporting you as you work to attain your goals as a model. You may also need to re-evaluate a lot of friendships because of this.

- At the start of every day, look in the mirror and find 3 things that you like about yourself. It could be your stunning complexion, your strawberry blonde hair, or even just the purple shade of nail polish that you chose this week. You have to praise yourself every so often; otherwise no one else will praise you.

- One of the dirtiest tricks that photographers and agencies do with models is to try to lower the model's asking price by insulting their looks, their portfolio, and anything else that they can think of. As terrible as this practice is, it's sadly a very common thing for freelance models to face in their day to day lives.

Should you feel that you are being victimized by these tactics, simply take a break and shoot with photographer friends who actually do realize what you're worth. You'd be surprised at how quickly people will ask for you by name.

• You have to act like a model, as well. This means that you will have to act like you deserve the shoots that you get. You have to convince the photographer that you really are a no-brainer for any project that he may have.

Should you ever find yourself in a position where you can't get yourself to feel comfortable in a shoot because of a photographer's behavior, just leave. Believe it or not, you will probably doubt yourself for 5 minutes, but will thank yourself 5 months later. It's surprising how quickly you'll realize that standing up for yourself actually helps you keep your pride.

- Don't believe that every model shoot should be rated on money alone. There are plenty of models who basically sold their souls in order to become top models, and there have been plenty of such models who have been treated for depression, or even put on suicide watch because of their decisions.

  Money isn't everything, even if it seems like it is when you first get a real paycheck from your modeling work. Actually being happy with your modeling work is more important than any paycheck you'll receive.

- Lastly, never let anyone tell you that you're not a "real model." If people ask you for photo shoots, you're a real model. If people are asking you to pose for their portfolios, they are asking you to model for them. Don't ever let others sell you short of your true value. If they make commentaries like that, simply refuse to shoot with them later on. Believe it or not, they always come back.

Conclusion

Over the previous chapters, you have learned a lot about the modeling world. You have learned about the good, you have learned about the bad, and you also learned about the little things that most people never imagine that models have to do.

It's a lot to take in, and it's a lot to do in order to pursue a dream. However, dreams are dreams for a reason. Instead of thinking of your modeling career as a dream, think of it as a goal.

Unlike dreams, you can achieve goals. Goals are something to work towards, and in the modeling industry, hard work is the only way to become the next top model.

So, instead of daydreaming about walking down the catwalk next to Naomi, start walking down the catwalks in local shows. While others dream of having photographers shoot them for fun, you can actually be the girl in the next magazine.

The difference between being the girl who dreams of it while reading her magazines and being the girl looking back from its pages is action, pure and simple.

Even in other industries, you make your own luck. When it comes to the incredibly competitive industry of modeling and fashion, you can't expect a scout to walk by and give you their number. You need to start working in order to make yourself known.

And, the only way to do that is to book some shoots.

That being said, happy posing!